D1765905

AnimAls
in the
HOUSE

To Renée,
   In solidarity
with our love of
the earth + all
things wild!
         C

Animals in the House

poems by

Caryn Mirriam-Goldberg

WOODLEY MEMORIAL PRESS

© Caryn Mirriam-Goldberg
Autumn, 2004
ISBN 0-93939135-x

Cover painting and book design by Paul Hotvedt,
Blue Heron Typesetters

Woodley Memorial Press
Washburn University
Topeka, Kansas 66621

Printed in the United States of America by Lighting Source

The author gratefully acknowledges the following publications in which earlier
versions of these poems appeared:

Midwest Quarterly – "Landed," "Field"

The Literary Review – "Tricks of Gravity"

The Exquisite Corpse – "About Desire"

Mothering – "Telling My Son About His Birth"

Minnesota Review – "Telling My Son About His Birth"

California Quarterly – "Lightning, No Thunder"

Lullwater Review – "Happiness"

Higginsville Reader – "Leap"

Kaw: A Spoken Word c.d. – "Girl"

G.W. Review – "Girl"

Planet Drum Pulse – "Coordinates"

Willow Springs – "Jonah and the Tree"

Kansas City Star – "Spring Song"

The Phoenix Papers (anthology, Pente Press) – "Animals in the House,"
    "About Desire"

Lawrence Journal-World – "Magnolia Tree in Kansas," "Spring Song"

The William Stafford quote comes from Stafford's poem, "East of Broken Top,"
published in his book *Even in Quiet Places.*

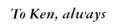

To Ken, always

Contents

What the Earth Holds

Animals in the House

. . . We lie on the earth;
to keep from falling into the stars we reach
as wide as we can and hold onto the grass.

— *William Stafford*

Tricks of Gravity

Girl

When I was a girl I didn't know
I was a girl. I thought I was
more of a pigment, a choral tone,
some kind of weather that disrupts
everyone's life in the living room.
I knocked over the cast iron iron again,
and this time it broke. How could
you break an iron iron? they yelled,
but how could I not? The weight of
metal on the earth, wanting to return.
When money was missing, I thought surely
I must have taken it.
When it rained, a hurricane this time,
I thought, see what you've done now.
I didn't believe in cause and effect, elements of
surprise, or the slim chance meetings
that changed everyone's lives. I didn't know
that people were supposed to end,
contained as vases to hold
whatever you gave them.

I thought we were more like land, islands even,
unfurling in the brown haze of the sea.
I thought there was water everywhere,
pouring us into changeable shapes –
leaf or puppy or branch. All falling
toward wherever we came from
not afraid or surprised,
not bad or tricked into good.

All falling back into the horizons that come
each evening to meet the fire.

Magnolia Tree in Kansas

This is the tree that breaks
into blossom too early each March,
killing its flowers. This is the tree
that hums anyway in its pool of fallen
petals, pink as moonlight. Not a bouquet
on a stick. Not a lost mammal in the clearing
although it looks like both with its explosions
of rosy boats — illuminated, red-edged.
Not a human thing but closer to what we might be
than the careful cedar or snakeskin sycamore.
It cries. It opens. It submits. In the pinnacle
of its stem and the pits of its fruitless fruit,
it knows how a song can break the singer.
In the brass of its wind, it sings anyway.
Tree of all breaking. Tree of all upsidedown.
Tree that hurts in its bones and doesn't care.
Tree of the first exhalation
landing and swaying, perfume and death,
all arms and no legs. Tree that never
learns to hold back.

Tricks of Gravity

What was surprising was the quiet.
The neighborhood in twilight, the blood
coming out some part of my face,
even the streetlights so familiar
as if I hadn't just crashed into a row of cars.
Honeysuckle the only sound
through the open windows of my car.
Just like longing, I knew then,
a scent you want, you want
but lean into and it's gone.

When they pulled me from the car,
said, say your name,
I said yours, wanting so much
I didn't know I was hurt.

Hours later, on the pull-out sofa,
all the bandages in place,
we lay on our sides facing
into that honeysuckle everywhere.
A gravity. An inevitability. I knew
I could never not turn this way,
and if I did, I could never not want more.
A crashing you hear the moment before impact.
So we pressed together once
in that ache that comes
right after an accident when no one knows yet
how much damage gravity does
to the world all the time.

What I Want From You

Can't you see me sitting cross-legged
on the blanket in the high grass
waiting for you?

Can't you see it's almost frost
and I'm naked? Take off your clothes
and come here, down inside this field.
Talk to me with the longness of your
legs and arms, shortening around me.
until we're just one fallen round thing.
Say what you can with your hands,
and when the wind blows those words away,
kiss what is left.

Your lips balanced on mine —
the silk of one life pressed into another.
This holding, turning I will not even be sure
when you enter me or when one
then the other of us falls
right through the seam of the sky.

About Desire

1.
Northern lights! So we grab our baby and run north. When we stop, our breath hardening in the air, he says, we made a mistake. It's only fog over the airport lights. But it's still amazing, he lies.

2.
In the good dream I lean my hands on the kitchen table where my great-aunts eat cheesecake with cherries. I squat slightly. Now labor can begin, but instead the baby's head crowns. I pull it out by its shoulders and tell the aunts, it's a girl. Well that was easy, they say, but why aren't you wearing any panties?

3.
Even this far south, in our neighborhood once, with everyone in the middle of the street, t.v. guides under their arms, pointing up and staring, we saw the red flare across the stars. We saw it move.

4.
In the bad dream a man with food in his beard says, it's a miscarriage. He spits tobacco on the floor, whispers, and it's your fault.

5.
Desire is like dust, the bodhisattva in the bathroom says. Put it in a certain light, it becomes what you yearn for.

Dust on the atmosphere and you get northern lights, an illusion of the divine when really god forgot to vacuum.

6.

Sometimes I go for walks with the baby and his stroller. While he points to every light fixture and says, moon, I feed him the cherries I just bit the pits from. He points to cats and laughs because they're all his. We're happy.

7.

Once, almost asleep, I wanted a lover so much I invented one: tall, muscular, brown hair and blue eyes, all compassionate so he weeps into my hair for my loneliness. This is what Jesus must be like, I thought, but then again, why not the best?

8.

I sit on the grass and cry. The sky is clear, relentless with stars, the grass dry and noisy. He lays out his jacket and unbuttons his jeans. The first baby's asleep, he whispers, let's make another.

9.

In the worst dream I live alone in a tenement, eating soup from the can, cold, and watching reruns of *The Beverly Hillbillies*. I want nothing.

10.

Last week the stomach flu made me lie down and watch flutters of white leaves fall. The train's whistle every half hour turned into an all-knowing animal who would answer any question I had of the universe. After all the aspirin in the house I still couldn't stand it so I got up and vacuumed.

11.

In the best dream of all I'm awake and can ask anything: what is god? may I have an orgasm now? am I pregnant? make cheesecake materialize. And the answer — always the same — is a picture of the planet with a red arrow pointing to a glob of green next to a sign flashing, yes, you are here.

Leap

The light around the tree returns
to say it never left.

It returns to say it sees me
still a girl in a pale yellow dress,
white socks ringed with dirty lace,
black patent leather shoes already scuffed.
There, at the base of a tree
trying to make language
out of the way I move my fingers
to call the light back.

But it never left.
It was only the volume of the world's language
turned up, those flippant slaps accompanied
by rushed vowels and faded patience

while I was caught in the blue rapture
of bird-like shapes of sky
made by leaf bent over branch,
while I was caught dreaming of standing very still
on the third-story ledge of an old school
just before I'd leap

into that space between things
words named away from me,
into that world not yet damaged
in my small body.

What I Could Tell

I could name all the pieces of violence —
the kick or slap, the friendly punch.
"Say it again," the therapist says.
I remember this later, lying in the bathtub
watching my arms and legs float in water, so normal.
Do you see how contained I am? How calm
a poem, as if I were writing about
tree limbs in winter covered in ice. Delicate.
Connected to the glass trunk, bone to bone.

I startle awake. Someone behind me. Reflexes
not everyone has anymore or ever.
But that was another time, weighted in
the cells of skin. Smoke in the vein of the bone.
Does it matter that the shelf of sky was blue,
that there was heat right where
the fist imprinted itself on my leg?
Did it happen like a shovel edge into roots,
someone watching, hands around my neck
before I could speak, and I'm dying
all over again?

There was a room with no air, a cringing
inward, the iris already broken from its bulb.
There was a bathtub with a girl covered
in bruises, the door locked hopefully.

She was tired, so tired
she couldn't stay awake
to tell me what really happened.

Fly Over

Nothing so careful as what is afraid.
Think of the hummingbird on our way
to the airport. Fire green, mid-air
until it sees us. Or last night
how I carefully folded myself
to sleep away from you
as if the small heat in your palm
could hurt anyone.

Suspended 30,000 feet on this plane, I try to imagine
you as someone I actually live with for years
but all I see is the curved spine of mountains
eaten round by air, the spilt milk of salt
on the desert's floor, the plane's shadow
pitched ahead of itself, miniature
in its future.

Nothing to add up and understand.
You, hundreds of miles behind, driving home
on the worn tracks of the earth we know by heart
to where, exactly a week from now,
I'll lie beside you in our bed.
Never the faint lines of a scar
where we joined together long ago,
almost healed, a new creature,
but always the opposite:

Your hand cupping my forehead before I'm awake,
I remember how broken I am
but turn toward you anyway.
Now, here, suspended between flight,
the beating of wings,
our eyes open mid air.

Half-Things

Look at the tree one way, and it's whole,
but the other half is cut away for a power line
like the car I totaled – one side perfect
so you could sit in the driver's seat,
look straight ahead, everything fine
except the plush of the passenger door
leans in just a little.

I was like this. I showed my broken side
to the mirror and said, this is all wrong, all wrong.
I was a half-thing who memorized sheet music
and the blossoms of orange or purple on my arms
from walking into table edges, door frames, fists.
Outside the rain fell so hard it bounced when it hit
the sidewalk. "Get away from the window,"
my grandmother screamed, "it's almost a hurricane,"

but I wasn't really afraid
of thunder, the surprise of lightning
even when I told myself I wouldn't be surprised.
I knew there was a slight sheen of muscle
in my arm when I flexed it, and a tree
right outside the window
whose bark curved slightly as if
ready to explode round again.

Happiness

for Daniel

I knew happiness in one continuous motion
the moment the midwife held up a knife and cut me,
everything shining and breaking. There, pressing
against the window, the cottonwoods that would frame
your childhood, rushing toward us in leaf and wind.

In the dark branches skinned white and peeling
I was just like you, clanging all over inside.
"What's wrong with you, you stupid schmuckhead?"
my father would ask. And my mother, "Remember
to try to make friends." I was your age, Daniel,
friendless, so they took me in the taxi
past the singular birches to see my first shrink, trembling
that the first child didn't understand something vital
about how to glance at the world.

What did I need with the world when I had the tree?
Its legs mined the earth for water,
the very book of happiness, opening
up the spine of each rounding leaf.
Then the wind that would not control itself –
always a miracle, a miracle
to watch no matter how long I waited
from my seven-year-old window,
all the bruises on my arms and legs solitary,
the belt my father used for this
demilitarized on the floor. I was actually happy
and nothing could undo that.

I was actually drowning in happiness
for hours, the leaves, but mostly the trunk
that let them go with such generosity
and tenderness, with such faith

that I felt a hand cupping my forehead,
a miracle singing at the window,
hold me throw me hold me against myself;
at the very center of the trunk,
a thousand green eyes
swimming in a school of green fish
back to the rivers
underground.

Overground, you wake and come sit with me
at the window while the trees
link us, hand over hand of the leaf,
into some tangled branch of happiness
shuddering or lifting slightly
at the slightest breath.

The Wishing Tree Talks

Not so hard to lean back against me,
like falling asleep. Like falling off
a cliff but then it was only a dream.
So lean back. Watch how the world looks
from inside my cupped leaves.

What are you waiting for?
The lip of storm to climb over?
Your thoughts to stop?

Sit down. See how the cusp
of my smallest branches
shadows the gray bluebird.
Watch the wind pour across
your crossed legs on its way to me.
Hear the crickets open the air up
with their wound. Lean in.
Nothing outside of yourself
will hurt you here.

What hurts in the folds of valley,
the bare parts, the rocks?
In the torn ledge of hill,
in the black of the black-eyed susans,
in the curl of breath out of the visible?
It is all the earth dreaming itself
at a speed that would toss you off
if it were not for gravity,

so then it's all gravity.
Sit back down. Look at me.
Have you forgotten what you need to forget?

Landed

Here everything is a list of its details:
the surface of crow feather where it bows,
or echo of whippoorwill through the closed window
over the bed. The chiggers and the slow-creeping
cedar trees, milkweed webbed with spittlebug,
and the grass above and below ground,
mirroring out from a single point
of root and longing.

I'm landed here, in the center of something
not my own doing, and although I keep thinking
I'm alone, I'm dying, I'm afraid,
I'm making all that up.
The man I love is coming out of the woods,
the long crescent of his body closer, bowing to touch
something, say its name.

When he stands back up, he walks slowly to show me
whatever we think of love is just the aerial view
that tells you nothing compared to the soft green stems
that curl and fall with the wind, compared to how each step across
the grass is a form of falling
out of and into what losses make life possible.
The quick flashes, like the sun balancing
on the lip of the horizon right before
it goes out, like that moment the field golds
everything opaque, like how love strips us
out of the stories we have for love.

The Dark
Between the Stars

Imagine You Know How to Fly

In fact, you've done it all your life –
the view from above always multi-textured, dense,
promising more than close-ups.

Like in this field, late winter, the baby green dissolving
in the wet field like watercolors.
Up close, the deer's contoured belly, muscles
straining against the underside of fur.
See how it breathes?

Now fly forward – to the edge
of late summer, just a few fireflies
diagonally making their way up
through the white air to blue air.
Drop your arms and stop fighting.

Leave your house behind you.
Go to the wind pouring over and under
the ledge of the sky.
Jump in.

Coordinates

I live just south of the poetic,
where the glaciers stopped short, sloped down
to nothing. Now low-flying catfish line
the brown rivers while the valleys go flat
as clavicles edging into erosion and horizon.
The grass, obsessive as always,
runs itself oblivious,
and the cedar trees wave,
one arm, then another,
as if under water.

I live where the sky, dense and
exhausted, complains all smug and blue
that nothing ever happens here,
and leans asleep on its elbows in the corner.
It dreams what we mean: that we can only
locate ourselves in the weather that maps us
but can't be mapped ahead of itself.

Here there's no way to know what's coming,
or what's gone, the big bluestem being as tall as it is.
The wind comes. The wind goes. The sun climbs
around the corner and returns at its appointed time.
The windows shake in the storm that can pick up a field,
undress it, place it back down.

When I try to say where I am, I can only
point to the rushing everywhere
the mind tries to be still,
and in that wind, the stillness
that holds a single glance of switchgrass
up to the light before letting it go.

Kaw River

This is how I fell in love with you.
Not because the river was a metaphor
of good and bad intentions,
not because it carried the world past us
but because it was the world.

I leaned on the bridge support
to kiss you on the catwalk
while the roar, broken in gaps
by concrete pillars, pushed around
and back together.
I looked at you and said, okay,
this will be our life.

This is where we'll return to fight
and cry, to climb the bank in winter
or sit our babies on the sandbar
and dig circles around them.
This is where we'll watch the high water
with the crowds on the bridge in the flood year,
where we'll sit on the silk sand after losing
your grandfather, where we'll walk the drought sand
all the way across to the buried island, listening
to the river say:

I wind around weather and floating cars.
I'm a strand of pearls without the pearls.
I carve rain and run creases in clouds of snow
to curl around the rocky ledge, the single cottonwood,
the diving birds and rushing logs long broken from home.
I am a holder of running pollen, river of screaming light.
River of cardboard catfish and moving trees. River of wanting water.

And in the dark, a black velvet river: fire on the sandbar,
two people holding each other, flame pulled up to the clouds,
down into the mirror of the water, a spring of blue fire
that burns itself into being.

Almost Totality: Partial Eclipse

This is how I would want it between us:
the edges of your hair so separate
from the sky, the muscle
in your forearm so contoured
and distinct from the lanky hill in the distance,
and your words, clearly delineated
from mine, concentrated not on reaction,
but casting a million slivers,

the crow so still in the mowed grass,
the absence of wind, the carved shadow
of a gesture on a parked car,
the face half-turning back
to hold cardboard up to the sky and see
the end of the world
or the beginning.

Your face looking at the sun no longer
so dangerous, past almost totality
as your clothes follow the lines
of your body, the muted grass mats
in the wind, your arm lifts slightly
to touch my back like a tree branch
and I can't tell anything
that makes us separate.

The Dark Between the Stars

Lyra climbs the roof, a splattering of constellation
translated into a shape we can name.
See the teapot of Sagittarius, the Northern Cross,
and that ankle dangling from invisible hooks
in the milky way.

We stand in the yard and point, you behind me,
an oversized shadow of heat and shade.
See the dark between stars where nothing seems to be?
Even there, galaxy piled upon galaxy,
and at the same time, the space between the nothing.
Later, when we can't keep our eyes open anymore,
sleep tumbles over us. A falling open of archway and air,
a phone ringing, then the phone turned into
a cotton sheet flapping outside all night
against the hard sky.

I wake dreaming in multiples of nine that correlate
to lakes spilled across the grid of the Midwest.
The weight of everyone's wounds in a particular town
where the dull pain fountains so smoothly
you don't realize it's pain. Everything rushing apart in random or-
ange dots, the fibers of the eye, something that sounds like an owl
in the dark, like the screech of a car

and nothing, not drinking a glass of water
or turning on the light, can keep me from sleeping
right back into this dream of infinity
well below the shapes skies make,

the curve of the forehead
that holds in the brain, the slope
of hill in the distance
that mimics the horizon
so all I can do is wake you, say, tell me
how to undream this, tell me the names
of these constellations that won't stay
still enough to name.

You fold your legs under my knees,
place your open hand on the side of my face,
and say, the opposite of infinity
is love.

Three Walking Songs for the Night

1.
I walk across a field. No more destination,
journey through or over water.
No more dreams of arriving.

I'm here, overlooking a small slope
that leads nowhere. Leaves drop out
of the wet branches. The field eats them.

A fox. Then the sky turns itself
like a clever hand this way and that,
blocking or letting through the moon.

Sometimes rain falls. No matter.
The animals come anyway.
When it clears, I lie on the fallen grass,
look at the brave sky,
and tell myself, "shut up and trust that."

2.
When I wake in the dark, I will go to the forest
with no flashlight, and walk slowly, afraid,
letting my feet make out where next to step,
waiting for what's hidden to let me into its hiding.
No longer dreaming of his hands cupping my head
tenderly, I will just walk in, feeling only
where to land, the noise of the running world no longer running,
the tree frogs cupping their motor song over
the motor song of the cicadas, the brush of branch
on branch, the owls a broken harmonic.

Oh, dream of being loved so perfectly,
Oh, dream of forgiveness,
Oh, damp moon in a pool of clouds,
wide stillness of nothing that we call sky,
now, please let me be brave enough.

3.
I was afraid most of that year.
No particular reason.
Just the rush of old air through my lungs
as if it had nothing better to do.

I'd wake a lot at night, puppy diving
after the kitten, the baby nightmaring
right into the center of my good dream.
I'd wake for nothing also,

sit up, climb out of bed, walking the house
to prove to myself there was no reason
to be afraid. I mean, look at that moon
carrying itself branch to tree branch.
Look at the indentations the wind makes
of its body in the grass.

See how round the earth is,
remember how many animals sleep
hidden like prayers in the tall grass.

See the open mouth of the sky, the shifting of stars
across the throat of the universe,
this time in its slot actually happening.

Birthing Room

The pain annihilated me
in 20-second intervals
while people watched, trying
to think of something to do.
I watched the diagonal light
of the window blur colors. Meanwhile,
there was the power of the body to reckon with,
a gorgeous mountain in storm,
a crushing animal on its hind legs
inhabiting an ordinary woman, unaware
she was in a room of death
where the sun hung inside-out,
and somewhere, a baby
was trying to use her lungs.

Ask me about it now
that my daughter is old and large,
and I'll tell you how I was the only one in that room
who could hand her out the open window.
I was the only one outside who could catch her.

Lightning, No Thunder

Across the diagonal of the house
my son sleeps in his own sweat,
a good sign, I tell myself.
A show of fire fleshed through
the pores of the body
after nights of high fever.
"Nothing I can explain," says one doctor.
"It doesn't make sense," says another.
They shrug toward a virus, an animal
not alive, a thing
not dead.

Tonight I sit outside on a bench
in the center of the trembling
sky. Heat lightning all directions
the trees don't mask. Occasionally
a strand of fire pulled down
and under into that far away dirt.

Last night I carried that big
eight-year-old boy to my bed,
all night my hand on his forehead
while the heat charged his skin. But this
is the earth too, the very substance
beside me as I sleep,
there asleep in that turning
while I sit right outside his whole life
and ask the sky,
Please.

What the Field Says

How is it you should love,
you who cannot say the word
without forgetting it is not yours
to keep silent as fallen leaf under foot.
How will you tell me what it means to sing?
What it means to stand in perfect silence,
and sing as loud as you can?

How do you presume to speak for us?
We who filter wind as regularly
as you exhale, we who hide
all things made of fur
and engine hearts.
We who throw our lives
down without a thought,
who fling open at the roots
and cry in love with
the wind, the wind, the wind.

What do you even know of the wind
when your body can hardly ever
split apart, open at the seams
and pour back into a whole field
of singing grass?

What Would Happen If You Walked Here?

What would happen if you opened to something
so totally beyond human that it dissolved your borders
into bluestem? What if it rained and you got wet?
What if you understood not just that the earth tilted
but that it tilted right through your spine
and that's why you occasionally fall over?

Nothing prepares you for the real.
There's no journey out of this except the one
that separates your bones from your thoughts,
your tendons from the lines of your desire.

In the giant mouth of the dark,
in the opening screen of the dark,
in the bottom of the pot of the dark,
is the dark that isn't so dark.

In the myriad call of meadowlark layered on siren
of coyote upon clanging of wind in cottonwood tree
is also the sound of no sound, too.
Nothing can prepare you for the speed of the universe.
Nothing can steady you enough to absorb even the fact
that light travels millions of years to get to your eyes,
that the dissolved dust of stars are your thoughts
and your thinking, that the sky is so big, that the dirt is made of
bones and breath, that there's nothing heavier than the ocean,
that there's no such thing as exact replicas in the seasons,
and that seasons pour through us like rain or dust
whether we're paying attention or not,
that a rabbit can outrun you in your prime, that language
is only partially made of words, that the earth cannot help
but to keep recycling you into something better.

Conversations with a Cedar Tree

I. Speaking to the Cedar Tree

"This shaking keeps me steady – I should know."
— Theodore Roethke

When I lie beneath your canopy,
asking the dirt below for help,
I realize you're already pointing
no actual direction, careful and careless,
your slimmest branchings humming
with something we could call pain or death
and that sweet scent, old and boney,
knotted to another world.
The smell of dark blue.
The hazards of your edges.
The hollows of you full
of chirp and flutter. A shaking steady,
a way to hold gravity and make it visible
without holding it still, a dance
of tangle, bird call, fear, sweetness,
all the glory strung bone to stem,
all contained in this one dark candle.

II. The Cedar Has Its Say

I'm that dark container for birds,
explosions of mating songs
or death songs — I can never tell —
whittling through me day and night.
In the summer, I can hardly hear myself think.
Ghosts of blue diamonds of sunlight, wind shaking
the shadows that know how to
inhabit me, hide under the seams,
nothing but air with its long list of travel plans.

Everything you touch on me can hurt you.
That's just the way I'm made.

In the winter, I'm buffered by snow, or its absence,
chiming with the smaller birds who hop, interior branch
to interior, a city of ecstatic synapses
while the rabbits dart into my white center,
lean on my main root, breathe hard.

I'm a tree, but I can imagine what it is to smell coyote
or bobcat while the swollen flanks of pregnant deer
brush against me. Meanwhile, the dark green you see
is actually made of fire meeting dirt.
The open ache you feel when you hold your hand above a bough
is what all loss feels like when made solid.

Burning the Prairie

1.
A field is a black hole, shadow made solid
fastened to the ground.
The skull of a baby deer lies there
in the old black hair.
The closed entrance to a mouse house
in dirt that filters sunlight
like the heart filters blood.
I stand on the field's ledge, think about the past,
charred only where I've touched it.
The stories of one slow burn or another.
How much water is there in the world anyway?

Not enough, says the inside of a cave.
Not enough, says the snippet of lilac in the bedroom.
Not enough, says this field.

2.
Years ago, my husband was burning a field
when the field started burning him back.
Caught in the change of wind
clanging the flames closer so they could do
what they long to do most their whole fire life
– rush up a huge sheet of brilliance –
he did the only thing to save his life:
he ran through the fire.

3.
A duck cries. I dream I'm standing
in the burned field again, but before it was burned.
I don't like all this tangle and height.
I want the future cleared away,
absent and present at once.

4.
We burn the field so the grass
can have its house back,
clean out the houseguest-from-hell trees,
sweep the floors, open the windows
to let the smoke out.

We burn the field so that we, ignorant to the black sky,
can see sheet after wavy sheet of burning,
and call it beauty.

We burn the field to start something we can't stop
and then stop it.

5.
After the burn, I hold my husband's hand
in the bedroom like it's a candle
I wouldn't want to tip toward
all that's dry, all that's above ground.

No one talking, the dark as heavy
inside as it is out, the ceiling fan swooshing
us still. I am scared to lie here with the wind
so high, the tangle and brush of us ready.

How easy to start a fire.
How untrue that ripeness comes only
to the wet and lush.

What Do You Believe In?

The wind across the road and the tumbleweed
that follows it, the night and the stars,
the last coherent thought, and especially
what comes next. A hand on my shoulder.
The wooden stairs bare and wanting carpet
from the house where I grew up leading
to the one where I live now, my mother's laughter
on the phone, the sudden falling in a dream
before waking, the dark made by thing on thing,
the chance smile of a stranger on a side street,
my youngest son's hand in mine as he leads me
down the hall, the cranes stenciling the sky behind
the one leaf just breaking from the tree, all the trees
that turn light into something else, a bluebird quick
past the window, a secret pond to gather at
in our dreams, all manner of water,
arms wide open, breast plate leading
into the wind, a lifting of the uncontainable
out of the contained.

Daniel's Dream Speaks

I have always been here, perched on the shoulder
of the dark just where the body tumbles to sleep,
and the mind stops its venus-fly-trap lurches.
Or for some, right on the ridge of the teeth
that can rip apart flesh, fur, bones
as easily as daylight rips aside the sweet shadows
that envelope us.

For Daniel I stoop slightly, stretch out my wings
and launch across that divide to show him
cattle grazing in multiples of seven,
dramas of kings played out in garments and famines,
sweet figs hollowed with dry heat to leather.

"Listen, Boy," I tell his open ear.
He turns toward me, not the least bit reluctant.
"Terrible things will happen, and there's nothing
you can do."

Meanwhile, lions curl at his feet with no fear.
Meanwhile he dreams of women with browned skin
and lips like small, unopened roses
who gather in the secret field,
arm in arm, singing the clouds into being.

Telling My Son About His Birth

It was like visiting a house
I'd only seen before between sleep and waking.
I waited days to enter,
but once inside, I was afraid of the dark
and couldn't find the walls.
Maybe there was a storm.
I can't remember, only that I hurt and thought
I wouldn't get out.

I made noises.
Then I found you –
the top of your head black with hair.
I pushed and pushed to get out,
and when we did, into the hot room
where your father and the midwife waited,
I realized I was afraid most
because this house was the world,
and it was on fire.

But you need to know
there wasn't really a house at all
or any shelter. There was a place I cannot name.
You could call it fear or love
or god – it would still be the place
of no place.

Here, there is a real house
made of wood and concrete.
We have names for things
and a name for you.
We think we are past the fire,
asleep in this chair,
your belly on mine
as we breathe on each other.

Jonah and the Tree

You don't say you love that tree but you do.
Are you like this with anything
that gives you food or shade?
Oh, all of you get more rattled
at the sound of my voice in your satiny throats
because you're afraid of how stupid you'll look.

But I come to tell you
compassion always looks stupid
to those well-fed in a shady spot
while time bakes the earth.

Love looks stupid, too
as if the lover had no more sense
than to fling herself into the blank sky
she would soon fall out
like you, Jonah, back to the land
where a tree may mean all
because it makes you the god of it.

But if you lie there long enough
in the rain, you will remember how
the wet ground stretches itself open,
makes earth and sky the inside of a whale,
night unrolling into day,
day unrolling into night
in its old migration
back to me.

Once you can have gone so far,
how can you not let others return?

What The Earth Holds

Swimming in Mombassa at Midnight

I swam on water that must move
to keep its balance,
each stroke of my arms
making the whole pool rush
over itself again.
I swam in the quiet of faint television light
leaking out over the water, the swoosh
of taxis a block away,
while I stared at the moon, asking,
what will it be,
and how will it happen?
Clouds smoked past, a young Kenyan girl
carried the empty Coke bottles
back to the store for us.

And nothing happened. The wind
came and went. The trees paused.
The pool stayed cemented
in the crescent of thick dirt
encased by the Indian ocean.

The earth remained round
so that birds of the next day
could sing as if this life
were almost over,
the next one could now begin.

Hills Climb the Sky

for Laurie

Bill dead a year, I sit in the Mexican restaurant
with Laurie who looks more and more like Bill
crying. So how can he be gone? Laurie in the house
the day after he died, helping me dust c.d. cases.
Laurie in the new house, his picture everywhere, his note
in the recipe box suggesting the garlic dip.
Laurie in his chair, his shirt, and yet all around her
the weather orbits past, outlining how alone she is.

The earth turns on its axle when really
there's no slash of line through the center. Nothing
but fire, rock, underground rivers.
Still, he's not here at each tilt through each anniversary,
each night that rises up from the west while
hills climb the earth in their solitude,
arm in arm with each other yet rolling
alone into shadow.

A year behind the hills, there was a slope of tall grass
where we stood, Bill's ashes all over our fingers
like rain or powder. In the small sway of grass,
60 or so people freezing anyplace we didn't touch,
we spread what was left into the climbing wind
and let the turning of the planet do the rest.

What the Earth Holds

Somewhere Mongols paraded heads on sticks.
Blood moved through dirt like rain.
Cambodians, shot in the back,
dove out of their bones.
And Jews in the gas chamber looked up, stunned
for a moment.

These deaths only seem to evaporate.

The massacres charted in history books,
the massacres we don't know of,
drowned children, buried alive old men,
strangers hanging from branches
in the distance, even the private murders of cavemen
shape rocks, feed trees.

Here, for instance, the deep tangle of big bluestem
and switchgrass surely roots through dirt
that once filtered the blood of the Kaw tribe.
Valleys once blanketed with skulls,
all fever trees now. The bones that bleached
into oblivion, the teeth, the shadows staining sidewalks
all dissolved into dirt and dahlias.

The earth holds it all, more than the mind can imagine.
Meanwhile, our own bodies still warm,
all their weight to love because of and despite
all the skin unwrapped in all the mud,
all the green that still comes.

What the Sky Is Made Of

The sky is made of planes that can fall out as suddenly
as unexpected snow, right in the middle of houses linked
to other houses and matchbox backyards.
Someone you bumped into at an airport snack bar
could be dead now, even if he was kind enough
to share his newspaper with you.

The sky is made of soft rain and hard light
along with that old wanting to hold something
you can't name or never met, that fountain of wind
that says, something's gone, something else is arriving.
The sky is made of rocks shattered so finely
they're smaller than the smallest atoms
of the human heart, air we call breath once we take it in
and give it a tour of the body. The sky is made of change
and the flux of water held away from its own weight
so it can become something else.

The sky composes itself not of danger or safety,
not of relentless sorrow, but of something
much finer, far less predictable: the beating of
a hummingbird, for example, the fluttering
of muscle on muscle, making the eyes ignite
as they look up and see what will fall next.

Accident Site

I try to remember holding the child
limp in my arms and bleeding.
The ice and snow making it hard
to carry him up the ditch, the upside down van
something out of a nightmare. The flash
of all loss flaring through my body
like a burn that would never end.

I try to remember that moment
he started crying alive again
despite the void, common and everyday,
in my brain that said,
here it is, all you ever feared.

Months later, after we returned
to the site to clean the broken crayons,
find the eyeglasses, lift carefully shattered glass
and carry it away, the tiny river at the bottom
had already widened into spring.
But the air still breathed me in, the ground
still held the indentation of the van,
the wind still rose to rush along crow wing.
The place made of ice had turned to verbena,
shock shifted into rain, its shape as ditch and stream
changing expressions daily
but always saying the same thing:
The world can open or not all the time.

Holly

1.
At my wedding she wore a bulky turtleneck
under her thrift store gown
and opened her throat
so the world could fall out
the center of her song.

No-one with a voice that strong could disappear.
No-one so prickly pear and granite.

2.
When Holly died there was no funeral.
The Christian Scientists had long ago stopped visiting
and praying hard for her to pray her way out.
She still believed.

"How can you stand this?"
I asked her husband two weeks before.
He leaned his head upon the refrigerator and the room
filled with humming.

"I can't."

3.
So many times I hated how you sucked the life
out of every room you entered.
In the toy department of K-Mart
you screamed how could I know anything,
I didn't have kids yet.

We fought into the pool supply section,
this crazed flare that we would never get past. Something
in the stomach, something in the chest.

4.

Ballet that wrecked your knees,
bookshelves made from cinder blocks,
puppet theaters from refrigerator boxes,
the huge god's eye dangling in mobile,
how you wanted to crawl in the closet
and birth your first child alone,
woolen caps you wore even in spring,
homemade ice cream served after
the macrobiotic dinner,
but you were not to be touched.

5.

When the first diagnosis came, when they had to cut
armpit to sternum while the baby drank pumped milk
and the sun floated one day to the next,
when the dozen pine trees you planted the summer before
moved their tentative fingers in the wind,
when the casseroles paraded through, when you let me
sit with you on the bed and look at the stitches
and later hold the baby up against the visible breast,
his little legs kicking lightly
in the ghost breast, when
was this really?

6.

I want to hear the catch
in the voice, the box of a note
that is anything but a box.
I want to stop feeling uncomfortable
with you undead in the room
telling me I hurt you.

I want to know this song that breaks the mouths
of humans.

The Speed of Life

My son shows me all his eight years at once,
his eyes like the studied pattern of a fossil,
his face grown through a tumble of water and air
from when I first saw him open his black eyes.
His eight-year-old self and his just born self,
and earlier, that almost imperceptible feeling
of something like paper unfolding inside me
all at once, time not a rocket from the past to the future,
from here to there, but time tipped over, spilled out
into the field, the grass first breaking the dirt
with a needlepoint of green, the cut shadow of leaf
on rock 158 million years old, the cockroach descended
from the exact model 250 millions years ago,
the meteor dissolved, the wind beaten in and out of lungs
even before there were lungs.

The outer bowl of the earth fitted perfectly
into the inner bowl of the sky,
my son in my hands the first time
all of him at once contained in two palms.

This is the speed life travels,
so fast, so immediate from all directions
that you can look to the stars
in this galaxy or way beyond

on the same imaginary level ceiling of the heavens,
that you can look at the field
and see all the new grass, old rocks, ancient insects
on the same imaginary floor of the earth.

But what is up close, what fills your hands this moment –
that is the only way we have depth perception.
The tapered valley below the ribs,
the rise of eyelash right out into space,
all the distinctions carefully placed here or there
so we can make age out of this earth,
so we can point at something
as if it's not moving.

Animals in the House

And only then, when I have learned enough,
I will go to watch the animals, and let
something of their composure glide
into my limbs; will see my own existence
deep in their eyes . . .
> — Rainer Maria Rilke
> ("Requiem," translated by
> Stephen Mitchell)

When my best friend died, I ran,
the sidewalk ending, the sidewalk beginning,
the streetlights coming on as I inhaled,
the dark trailing behind me as I exhaled.

I ran like I'd never run before, no resistance of air or muscle,
no places asking me to stop and enter.

That rhythmic landing and leaving again, the slight bumps
of small pebble or curb actually sped me up.
No longer afraid of hurting myself or getting lost.
Nothing but the lust for speed.

I ran because this is what animals in pain do.

* * *

I light the shiva candle, the white wax filling
the glass cylinder, and now a flame to tell me
my father was alive, my father is dead.

As if fire can make sense out of running water
like a fever that smears all the dreams into static.
I hold this candle and read the Braille of the heart.
An animal who has lost its way. A territory so new
I first have to grow eyes to see it.

* * *

We lie in bed and kiss, the kitten perched
dangerously by our heads, claws extended,
the happy dog hopelessly crying
because he's so in love with what hates him,
the loose redbird crashing into the window
again, and all the animals, microscopic,
all over the houses of our bodies.

I put my mouth on your mouth,
all the bones so well hidden under
these kisses. Your palms on my shoulders,
my thighs wrapped around your legs, the indentations
we make on the mattress, everything falling
toward another core of gravity
within the core of the earth. Which is
the man, which the woman? Who speaks
Spanish or Japanese in the next room?
I can't remember what we're doing
anymore. Water in water.
Animals circled around
the empty place in the field.

* * *

Each night, it's the dream of another house.
The room below the basement I never noticed before,
and at its most interior, a whole slew of rooms,
empty and lit, some even with balconies
overlooking underground rivers.

Sometimes, it's a small place – a third-story apartment.
Or a single room suspended in the woods,
hard to find except in winter when the openness
of the trees surprises us. One house is full of
horses instead of furniture, panthers instead of dogs.

When the doctor says, "you have cancer,"
I take notes carefully, amazed
at the smoothness of the pen on paper
when the ground dissolves,
the falling begins and doesn't end.

Just a small mutation, a creature growing
out of bounds. Cancer,
I say aloud, on the phone, into the quiet air
that surrounds me just before sleep,
as if I'm naming a house so horizontal
it's impossible to ever blueprint.

*   *   *

The losses mounting as the wheel
of the world turns day to night,
night to day, a childhood cardboard cutout,
the ways stars fan over us just so.
In the dark, the lightning bug caught
in the curtain. In the light, the baby
batting at floating dusk, laughing.

How many losses do you know?

The bear dead in its cave. The root
of wild onion sliced by the shovel
where we'll plant wild onion.
The larkspur no one human sees.
The rain frogs lose to tree roots under puddles.
How many lost animals climb the darkness?

*   *   *

I've thrown myself down for a life
and I would do it again,
not out of nobility or love
but because I can't help it.

Animals fold themselves into sleep,
give their breath to their young without knowing
anything but the heat under fur,
the beating, and between each beat,
the open fields where anything can happen.

I fell into that animal world,
and couldn't leave without first pushing
that first child out of me, my whole life
thrown against the light like a shadow.
All the sounds of one chase
or another, all the caught animals
taking air into themselves,
making it theirs, letting it go.

Spring Song

What is it to wake at night not watered down
in overdrawn voices from the day, to see the space
and not the figure in the space, to fall backwards
in a dream and realize it's a dream?
What waits, wet as fire, on the end of the line?
The rushing of wings, the billowing of thunderheads,
the crashing of car into lamp post, the slivering of bark
from tree, the waking suddenly for no reason?

Meanwhile, insects reproduce themselves like breath,
birds loosen the sky with flight,
stratus clouds streak across the moon,
kisses stop, and stones break apart
so easily that it's clear they've been cracked inside
for a long time. Each life a transference of water.
Each act just a way to move light around.

Even knowing this, why can't the heart stop asking?

Acknowledgments

This collection of poetry began in 1984 when I heard the writer Stephanie Mills speak of inner and outer wilderness at the first continental bioregional congress. I'm immensely grateful to the bioregional movement, through which I've learned and am continuing to learn how to craft a life in balance with the prairie.

Many fine poets have helped me conceptualize and revise the poetry here, especially Denise Low, who has worked with me on this manuscript for years, and Judy Roitman, Stan Lombardo, Jim McCrary, the late Holly Exner-Thompson, Trish Reeves, Joy Sawyer, the Squaw Valley Community of Writers, the late Jane Kenyon, Stanley Plumley, Sharon Olds, and Howard Levy. Thank you, Beth Schultz, for your enthusiasm and wise eyes. Woodley Press has been an important source and support for Kansas writers. I'm also indebted to Paul Hotvedt for his gorgeous painting and fine book design.

Thanks also to the places that sustained me in writing and revising these poems: Z's Divine Espresso, Milton's, La Prima Tazza, and the now-defunct Pywacket's. I also thank the institutions and organizations that have led me to poetry and the power of poetry to transform: Goddard College, the National Association for Poetry Therapy, the Kansas Area Watershed Council, and the Kansas Conference on Imagination and Place.

Finally, my gratitude and love live with Ken Lassman.

Caryn Mirriam-Goldberg is author of *Lot's Wife* (Woodley Press), the award-winning *Write Where You Are* (Free Spirit Press) and several other publications. Her poetry and prose have appeared in over 60 literary journals and anthologies, and have garnered several awards. She is also a Lawrence poetry slam and grand slam champion. She coordinates the Transformative Language Arts program at Goddard College, a master's degree on social and personal transformation through the written and spoken word. A certified poetry therapist, Caryn facilitates writing workshops for many populations, specializing in eco-poetics, mythopoetics, writing through serious illness, and writing for justice and social change. She received her Ph.D. and MA from the University of Kansas. Caryn lives just south of Lawrence, Kansas with her husband, three children, and many animals. For more information, please see www.writewhereyouare.org.

Paul Hotvedt is director of Blue Heron Typesetters and a painter. For more information, please see www.paulhotvedt.com.

Printed in the United States
22393LVS00001B/389